OUTDANCING THE UNIVERSE

OUTDANCING THE UNIVERSE

by Lauren Gilmore

ACCELERATED READER
LEVEL:
POINTS:
QUIZ #:

This book published by University of Hell Press.
www.universityofhellpress.com

© 2015 Lauren Gilmore

Book and Cover Layout by Vince Norris
www.norrisportfolio.com

Artwork by Claire Grubb

All rights reserved. No part of this book may be reproduced or transmitted in any form or by any means, electronic or mechanical, including photocopying, recording or by any information storage and retrieval system, without written permission from the publisher, except for the inclusion of brief quotations in a review.

Published in the United States of America.
ISBN 978-1-938753-15-2

For Jenn

TABLE OF CONTENTS

PART ONE
MY DAD'S FAVORITE SUPERTRAMP ALBUM 1
GOLDILOCKS 3
LIKE THE FROG SOUND 5
FROM THE HOUSE ON BELT 8
SAY GOODBYE TURTLES 10
AT THE RETIREMENT HOME, NO ONE SPEAKS 11
CHOKECHERRY 12
WHAT THE LEATHER JACKET MIGHT HAVE SEEN 17
GRANDFATHER RABBIT 18
ON MY TWELFTH BIRTHDAY 19
EMMA 20
MISSING IN SEPARATE PLACES 23

PART TWO
WHAT WE GIVE AWAY 31
VISITING HOURS IN BABYLAND 32
GAS STATION CIGARS 34
A CONVENTIONAL SUNSET 36
WHEN HE LENDS YOU HIS JACKET 38
WHAT HIS BUMPER STICKER MIGHT HAVE SEEN 39
THE PAST TWELVE MINUTES 40

PART THREE
THIS IS A LOVE POEM 59
LINES IN SNOW 60
WANDERLUST 61
ON THE WAY TO CALIFORNIA 64
LAURA 65
THE VANISHING ACT 67

MY ONLY SUNSHINE 70
IN THE SMOKE 72
ON SLEEPING ALONE 73
WHAT THE PARK BENCH MIGHT HAVE SEEN 74
COST TO DINE 76
CLIPBOARDS AND PILLS 77

PART FOUR
PLASTIC CUPS 87
LAST PACK OF CIGARETTES 88
AFTER A HALF BOTTLE OF KRAKEN 92
WINDOWS AS WALLS 93
A POEM FOR THE UNINSPIRED 96
HAMARTIA 97
SECOND DEGREE BLACK BELT 98
DUST ON THE FRAME 99
CRUMBLING ARCHITECTURE 100
WHAT THE WALLPAPER MIGHT HAVE SEEN 102
COMMUNITY COLLEGE 103
AND THE FEVER AND THE CHILLS 104
NOT ANOTHER GRIEF POEM 106

"Maybe, he thinks, it is like the Noh: whenever the script says *dances*, whatever the actor does next is a dance. If he stands still, he is dancing."

—Jack Gilbert, "To See if Something Comes Next"

PART ONE

MY DAD'S FAVORITE SUPERTRAMP ALBUM
for Kurt Olson

He doesn't have a record player anymore,
but needs the boxes of vinyls from our basement
anyway. My brother knows better, says, *Mom
doesn't want you inside*, and offers him
peanut butter crackers instead, passed through
the screen door in a plastic wrapper.
I am standing where the hallway tile becomes
cherry kitchen linoleum, staring at the clock
on the wall shaped like a cow. Her name is Mable.
She stopped working the second time he crashed into
her, and now she doesn't even try keeping track
of the hours. Time slips away from all of us like that.
Those records never made it to the pawn shop
down the street. They collect layers of dust,
but they don't spin, and we don't dance.

GOLDILOCKS

Grandma Rain pushed a wooden stool
to the middle of the kitchen at lunchtimes,

set out three bowls of noodles and broth
and spread butter over saltines. Our soup

was never too hot while my brother, sister,
and I listened to her read *Goldilocks*

and the Three Bears. The thin floral curtains
above the sink were kept open, so she could

look out and watch Grandfather as he rode
the big tractor-mower across the lawn.

Those days the sun bleached my hair,
tip to root, the same yellow as the walls.

Just like Goldilocks. From my upside
down spoon reflection, I could be her.

A trespasser in my own imagination, I'll
swing between extremities until I break,

splintering like the knobby legs of a too-
small chair. When the bears come home,

I won't run into the arms of daytime
rationality, like the real Goldilocks did.

Instead, I'll wake into another nightmare,
crawl to a corner near the middle of the book,

and wait in silence for someone to turn
the page, covering me with her thumb.

LIKE THE FROG SOUND

Merlin the cat croaked. *D-e-a-d*. The adults spell out the hard-sounding word so none of us start crying. We listen from our spots on the beige carpet because armchairs and couches are for people too old to sit on the floor. The ceiling fan keeps making me dizzy up above us and it doesn't stop spinning just because Merlin croaked. It won't even stop when we leave the room, unless someone reaches up and pulls down on its string. *Dead* is a hard-sounding word but *croaked* is okay. It's kind of funny, really. Like the frog sound. There is another cat (named Gizmo) here to keep us company. Gizmo is orange and almost croaked too, this one night when a car didn't see him shadowed against the asphalt outside. He came back alive but afraid of everything like me, and now he never leaves the yard. I wonder if Gizmo remembers what color Merlin was, because I don't. It's always too dark to see when I feel his little paws stepping across my chest, letting all of the air out of my bedroom. A shot of paralysis up over my spine becomes spiderweb tingles shaking me awake again gasping and, no, I don't want to play in this game of musical chairs where everyone has to lose. Even when all of the adults croak I won't get up and take their places. I'll close my eyes and no one will see me. I'll become beige like carpet and disappear.

FROM THE HOUSE ON BELT

My father married a woman who
smoked cigarettes and styled hair
for a living.

She once took up painting,
covered the kitchen table with
newspaper. My father hung

a tree she'd dressed in autumn
on the wall of their living room.
She showed me how to mix

shades of blue to match the sky.
Nothing is ever one color, she said.
Her face changed the night

she slammed the door
and all of the nailed picture frames
came loose. The imitation

calm surrounding their house fell
like a hammer. My father
moved into the spare basement

of some friends across town
in a room without any wallpaper.
We shuffled big boxes

down the stairs, found a new shelf
for his books and DVDs,

dusted off the ashtray. Later,

walking beneath a cloud of nicotine,
he'd tell me a story about the wind
and what it takes:

a painting of a tree he threw
into the field during a thunderstorm
just to watch the canvas bleed.

SAY GOODBYE TURTLES

I could never get the sheets
to lay flat, no matter how many
times Grandma Rain showed me.
She had hall closets full
of fresh linen, folded along
perfect creases. From the dresser,
rows of trinkets watched me
struggling. She collected turtles.
Glass figurines, hairpins, brooches,
earrings. I liked to pet their shells,
tell them they didn't need to hide.
They stopped trusting me
the afternoon we submerged them
in cardboard boxes of foam peanuts
and loaded them into the back
of a U-Haul truck. Even when they
were unpacked, placed on the
same shelf, in front of the same mirror,
they knew something was different.
They couldn't watch Grandma Rain
fold sheets anymore. A young
nurse started coming in to do that,
never getting it right.

AT THE RETIREMENT HOME, NO ONE SPEAKS

A grandfather clock with its chest still, like a frozen
pillar of salt. A well-oiled rocking chair
swaying without noise. My father on the edge of his

seat, about to ask for money or get up
to check the medicine cabinet for Xanax.
Like an arthritic finger, a flower's stem

points to where cement and plaster
meet sky, aching for the sun-caked dirt that
once housed its roots. The only sound is

my grandmother crying. Words fall away
from our tongues like
withered petals. We do not try to catch them.

CHOKECHERRY

Chokecherry bushes grow
along the driveway of the house
where I grew up. For years

my mom warned us they were
poisonous, until the day
her boyfriend snatched one,

chewed, spat, and told her
what it was. Then she took
to making pies and jams,

storing them downstairs in jars
during the winter. The first time
I saw what a woman looked like

once she'd been sucked dry
to the pit, I was
still looking at a girl over

the bathroom sink.
After that boy had buttoned
his jeans and gone home,

after I'd said *No*
after he said to show him
my breasts,

and the couch cushions
sank under our combined weight.

A chokecherry looks ripe

long before it is ready
to be eaten. We were kids.
I stared at my reflection,

letting the water run over
my hands for ten minutes,
wondering if the residue

left on the palm and wrist
he'd taken hold of
could ever come clean,

how much soap it would take
scrubbed over my tongue
to ever speak again.

After his desire had passed,
he collapsed
into my lips: a kiss so gentle

it could have been his first
if I didn't know it wasn't. I didn't say
a word, as I picked up my shirt

and bra from the entryway. For years
afterward, any well-intentioned
touch still shut my body off like a faucet.

I didn't say anything

and he made varsity football
and I learned fear

and another bird swooped

down to the cement and left,
carrying with it
another soft, red chokecherry.

WHAT THE LEATHER JACKET MIGHT HAVE SEEN

outside a coffee shop full of strangers
wind works against the shortness
of her dress
  a cold sigh   eavesdropping buildings

the warmth of chamomile and kindness
in place of a coffin

she wraps her hands around the mug
and forgets the sleeves she wears do

not belong to her dead father, her lover,
or even herself   sometimes

a cigar is a cigar no matter how
long its scent chooses to linger

GRANDFATHER RABBIT

In that hospice bedroom, where the oxygen masks and Johnny Cash tunes were working together to keep you alive, you asked me to write you a poem. I found a scrap of paper at the bottom of my purse, scribbled something about a rabbit, since that was your favorite animal. Your eyes lit up. *I'm going to take it with me*, you said. *Even if they don't want me to, I'll hide it in my pocket anyway.* No one asked who you were talking about, just kept mapping changes in your face. The next time I saw you—tongue and brain disconnected by morphine—all you could do was squeeze my hand. Softer and softer. Each breath scampering home without you. Back to the prairie. To those afternoons on your back porch, smiling ear-to-ear like the watermelon rinds we tossed out into the tall grass. To the slick farm sweat of Iowa, skin already callused like leather. The sun ripe on your back, beating down heavy as the quilt you'd kick to the end of the bed seventy years later, legs desperate to outrun themselves.

ON MY TWELFTH BIRTHDAY

It was me face-to-face with the daughter
of a grandmaster twice my size because

I was old enough to be in her age bracket.
She kicked me senseless all three rounds,

won the match, and jumped up and down
until her belt fell off. In the hotel room later

each tear was a spark plug coming loose.
Before I saw another tournament, I'd stand

in front of a room, have my hands and feet
slapped while being sworn at in Korean.

And in English, *If you don't get a gold medal,
do not bother coming home*. When I got it,

I saw something like a nod, silence
sweeter than any applause. The trophy

didn't have my name engraved
on the side, but I held it like an extension

of my right arm, down low, tucked to my side.

EMMA

She had two short pigtails, sarcasm, and a block of field brush behind her apartment complex perfect for adventuring.

Of course, when we found that old red ski pole leaning in the crook of a tree like a grandpa in a doorway, we fastened a piece of fabric at the top, held it out as a flag to the wind.

It became our symbol, transforming northside Spokane suburbia into another universe, one we named *Chasa*, a combination of our two favorite things: chocolate and salsa dancing. We filled notebooks with sketches of creatures who lived there, decided on their heights, weights, hair colors, whether or not they spoke English, if they were afraid of people.

That was the year she taught me to swing dance. Her mom was dating another cowboy. Her grandparents lived down the street with an in-ground swimming pool and soft carpets. We colored our lips red with popsicles, ate tuna sandwiches, drank straight from the hose.

Her dad lived forty minutes away, called too much, and couldn't walk. His house smelled like urine and chewing tobacco. When visiting, she had to be careful not to spill his bedpan carrying it to and from the bathroom.

My dad lived downtown, got high too much, and didn't always remember to pick up the phone at all. His house smelled like cigarettes and candles. Every other weekend, he cooked me red sauce and pasta, while I sat upside down in his black leather chair, air-trumpeting to Miles Davis.

When the MS won and her dad died, she got a Chase Youth Award for courage. I brought her homemade jam in a jar, and a card, and we went to a baseball game.

His funeral was outside. It was too hot. The sun kept getting in my eyes.

She said they were going to bury him with his cellphone, so when she got lonely, she could always call, listen to him on the voicemail greeting.

When my dad died just a few years later, she had already moved, the *Chasa* flag torn beneath the bulk of my closet.

My big sister Allie and I sat up all night, crying because we were tired of crying.

They don't give awards to the girls whose dads drank themselves to death.

His funeral was also outside, also too hot.

They said I could speak, if I wanted. I had nothing

to say. A mosquito bit me, then another. I didn't swat either of them away.

Emma probably doesn't wear her hair in pigtails anymore. But maybe we are still cut from the same cloth, like those letters superglued to that flag. Maybe we wake at the same moments of the same nightmares, kicking heavy paralysis like sheets to the ends of our beds.

I imagine she still calls him every now and then.

Some nights I can almost hear that long, low moan of a telephone, echoes muffled beneath the lid of his coffin, still ringing.

MISSING IN SEPARATE PLACES
after Mohsen Emadi

Another family moves into that house. It is summer.
Yellow paint, stained glass to frame views of the
prairie. My grandmother's fingerprints feather
dusted from the counters. The place is a mess.
Another little girl sits under the porch. A small,
moon-shaped ring on the lawn catches enough
sunlight to be reflected in her eyes. She slides it
onto her pinky, fitting her hand better than it did
mine on that afternoon when I threw a Frisbee and
the ring went with it, disappearing into field brush.
She doesn't notice its fake silver discoloring her
skin until she pulls it off, sets it down on her
dresser. It was the first piece of jewelry I owned.
My cousin bought it for me in Seattle. Once it
was gone I wept until my grandfather found me.
He put his wedding band onto my finger and told
me to toss the Frisbee again, at the same angle.
We followed the path of his ring with our eyes,
breathless, children calculating a coin flip: to
where it landed in a patch of grass by itself. As
he picked it up, I stared at the indent left behind
in what was still his lawn, before my grandparents
folded their lives into suitcases and were sent
away to a series of assisted homes, disintegrating
with each move like the layers of a nesting doll.
First her, then him, the time between turning
clock hands to wrenches. It is never summer. In
a few months, the year's leaves will fall onto our
family plot. Ten minutes from the edge of town. A

dirt road turning up like dust along the riverbed. They will cover the dates on the graves until it looks like everyone died in the right order. My grandparents didn't bury their son. There were no funeral speeches for the young. No smiles through tired jaws of pity while my sister spoke, her voice shaking. From a distance, every procession looks the same. Clean rows of salt pushed across chests of oak. I dream I can bend metal around my hands like rope. I only hide to cry in places where someone dead might find me. A locket hanging low around my neck like a shield, making up for all the love I couldn't find when it mattered. The girl looks and looks, and always misplaces the ring before it has a chance to be outgrown.

PART TWO

WHAT WE GIVE AWAY

The first boy I kissed tasted
like cigarettes and was the only kid
in my elementary school who'd
ever seen a Stanley Kubrick film.
Before he started sitting next to me
at lunch and on the metal playground
I heard him tell a friend of ours
that I was nice but on a cuteness scale
from one to ten, I was maybe
a six and a quarter. The first time
we broke up, he told me he would
always love me, just differently, and I cried
into a pillow for three hours. When
we got back together in the summer
before seventh grade, he listed
off the names of five other girls he was
seeing at the same time as me.
We didn't walk through the snow and talk
about *The Shining* anymore. Instead,
he had stories about drugs and carried
a lighter. Standing on the blacktop,
he slid his hands into my back pockets
and told me to kiss him, so I did.
Two weeks before breaking up with me
for the last time, he told me to send
him a picture of myself without
a shirt on, so I did, careful to keep
my eyes and stomach out
of the frame, as absent from
my own body as the ocean
is from a seashell.

VISITING HOURS IN BABYLAND

        Maybe it was neither a small town nor a big city
but somewhere youth shuffles on the edge of the dance floor,
unsure if they are ready to dance

but feeling the music more than anyone else in the room.
        Maybe we wandered through cemeteries in the small
hours of the morning, when it was just us and the eternally

at rest and the light beams of the night patrol we dodged
from behind bushes and trees. I clutched the elbows
of older boys, and let myself be led into the fog. We became

accustomed to the banshee cries of the birds
perched on tree branches, the whistles of dawn.
        Maybe we could never get ourselves as lost
as we wanted in that little black car, turning down every

street we didn't recognize, our music busting speakers.
        Maybe we always made it back in one piece,
not entirely relieved, the future
swelling inside of us only just becoming audible.

GAS STATION CIGARS

It is four o'clock in the morning and
        Adam's headlights cut through the
                heavy curtain of fog as he drives Sam

              and me to Sky Prairie Park. We pull
      into a gas station on the way where
I am too young and have to wait

alone in the car while they buy
        a pack of fruit-flavored cigars
                I hope will stain the air with colored

                smoke. Instead, our exhales, wrung
      out pale as dishrags, linger a few
paces behind us while we run

down the hill, feet disappearing
        under each step. They both graduated
                from high school last year. Adam is

                going off to college in the fall. Sam
      just got a job bagging groceries
at Safeway. This summer, through

a fog thick as our indecision
        I can barely see either of them.
                The thing about the roads on the

                prairie is they don't go anywhere:
looping back into the city after

expanding only four miles.

Every path leads away like our
        chins tilted up toward a heaven-less
                sky, yearning for what can't be tasted

                through cheap strawberry tobacco.
        We push phantom rings past our
lips between coughs, our voices

curving like those roads. Two months
        from now, on a clear September night,
                his bags packed in the car behind us,

                Adam will walk around to the passenger
        side door and ask me to kiss him goodbye,
with only the asphalt as witness.

A CONVENTIONAL SUNSET

A young boy kneels on the sidewalk,
plucks a wildflower out from a cement crack
and holds it up to the light.

The world breathes a sigh of relief
at its recognizable beauty. The flower is dead
but at least we know where it stands.

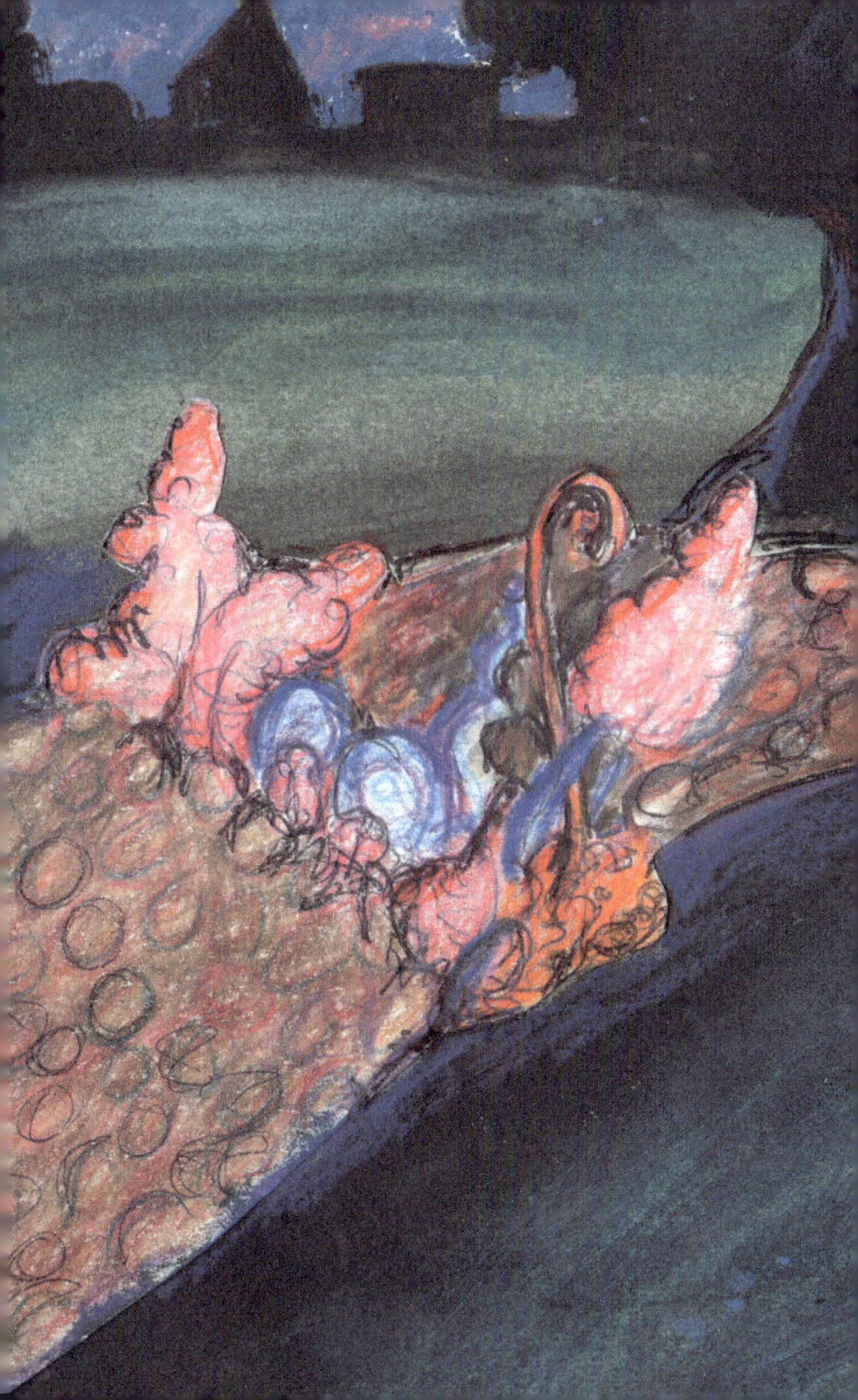

WHEN HE LENDS YOU HIS JACKET

You will no longer be on kissing
terms when he lends you his jacket.
The one with the name of a band
you tried to like because he did
printed on the back. You will be
walking together up Five Mile Road
and he'll point to the bed of a stranger's
lawn where you'll lay beside him,
careful not to touch. What once burned
between you will have settled into
ash, churned up by the inhale
of an evening too cold for its season.
Tugging the thin cotton of the sleeves past
your fingertips, you will cover each
patchwork silence with spools of empty
laughter and small talk. He will name
different landmarks on the horizon,
its lights dimmed into a string of pearls.
By the time you think to return his jacket,
he will have forgotten ever leaving it
with you: the entire month of July lifted
and tossed away like a piece of lint.
You will consider asking him about
first love, whether or not this counted,
through his rolled-down car window
before he pulls away to shake the
entire block with his stereo.

WHAT HIS BUMPER STICKER MIGHT HAVE SEEN

half-requited first love nightmares
of teeth falling out by the fistful
like missing piano keys his car

pulling away from a summer
of stealing kisses over the corpses
buried behind Joe Albi Stadium

shivering bathroom tile her hands
quiver around his absence she hums

her own lullaby rest rest
rest from the pages
of sheet music he left behind in her body

THE PAST TWELVE MINUTES
after Mark Anderson

12.

December. The midnight chime of a clock tower.
Everything starts and ends with the same sound.

11.

When death covers you like a blanket,
there will be twelve minutes between the surrender
of your prison-cell body
and the shutting down of your brain.

Like phantom pain
twitching across a severed limb
circuit board panic
denial
a   slow   motion dream   sequence.

10.

Welcome to the human race:
the only species masochistic enough
to keep track of time.
Wire red alarm clock digits
carve an unblinking tally into our retinas.

9.

East coast time zone discrepancies
a prematurely televised new year
the release of confetti doves
champagne crystal
engagement rings.

8.

When infinity is tipped on its side,
we can be certain: nothing lasts
forever.

7.

We want gift-wrapped swans
from a Christmas-song lover. Like
waterfowl, we must maintain
surface-level elegance
while paddling for our lives.

6.

And on that day, God created man.

5.

Children are born
instinctively gripping our thumbs
as guidance out of a fog recognized again
by the elderly. From morphine bed sheets
their wrinkled palms grasp.

Everything starts and ends with the same sound.

4.

And on that day
God created the sun,
moon, and stars.

What would life mean if it could not be measured?

3.

Galileo spent his final years under house arrest,
holding truth in a fist
the church could not pry open. Even today
his severed middle finger
    preserved and scrutinized
    from behind display case glass
    like a souvenir of defiance
points at something
the tourists
are unable to find.

2.

According to the Chinese creation story,
heaven and earth were once united
but gradually drifted apart.
If our hands should ever interlace again
              out-of-sight proximity
will be my excuse
for so much doubt.

1.

"And yet—it moves." Famous last words
are always debated and invariably
disappointing.

Even the noblest faith flinches
under the hand of mortality.

0.

Historians credit the Mayans
with the first mathematical interpretation
of nothingness, but often overlook

they chose to depict it
with the shape of our eyes.

PART THREE

THIS IS A LOVE POEM

       For three weeks before our first kiss
the maple leaves
above where you parked in front of my house
were ready to fall, but kept
clinging to their branches. You reached up,
felt the hemline of an auburn gown
one was arching its stem to fill, and said, *Almost*.

LINES IN SNOW

Outside of Snoqualmie Pass, cars pull over
to wrap chains around their tires but we have
four-wheel drive and keep climbing, chasing

our own sleet-covered tracks. His hand grips
mine tighter as the mountain ground starts
slipping underneath us and we spin. Staring

down the loaded barrel of an open road, my mom
says *Fuck* for the first time in her life and cranks
the steering wheel back into place, apologizing

her tongue away. It takes seven hours before
we're inside the house safely, her leaning against
the counter, filling our glasses with ice

and Chardonnay. With a fingernail chewed past
the tip, I trace designs in the condensation
on the wine glass. My knuckles look pale

for weeks to come, seeking out that same vivid
closeness: a traffic line of pale yellow, blinking out
my name as I drive, eyes darting back and away.

WANDERLUST

I.

The air above Tacoma, Washington is stamped
with pollution from the paper mill. Locals
are conditioned to not smell it anymore. It takes
leaving and coming back, like when my mom
loaded us into our blue minivan and we drove
across the state to watch her mother die.

On the bedside table, there was a laminated list
titled *Signs Your Loved One is Near the End*.
It included: They will speak of travel, without
destination. Just the concept of leaving. My mom
listened as Nana whispered frantically about
a red car parked right outside, ready to take her.

II.

On the night of my seventeenth birthday, I sat
in the downtown Greyhound station where the two-a.m.
bus would take me from Spokane to Portland.

My mom was sitting next to me, hands clenching
every time someone walked by, remarking under
her breath that she hoped *they* weren't getting

on the same bus as me. She grew up moving
across the Orient, never staying in the same town
for more than a few months. Her children

wouldn't be raised like that. I don't know when
wanderlust started collecting in my shoes like rain
in hurricane gutter pipes. Or why the only

place I have ever felt homesick is with my elbows
on my own kitchen table. I have always slept best
between mile markers. Every step

a miniature departure, I walked forward
into line with the other passengers, becoming
the same kind of no one as everyone else.

III.

Nana used to be a dancer. There are photo albums
filled with snapshots of her legs rising up from stage

floors under floods of lights. On Saturday mornings
she would call my mom and her little sister

out into the living room to do chores. This always
turned into Nana blasting the album *Whipped Cream*

by Herb Alpert's Tijuana Brass while she marched
around the house holding broomsticks like batons.

Two weeks before she died, Nana laid on her back:
head tilted to one side, surrounded by people

she had forgotten how to love. My mom set up
a small radio in the back of the room. Just to see

if anything could break through. A familiar song
spilled out from the portable speakers and her eyes

flipped like quarters into a jukebox. A hum escaped
her lips while she moved, the most she had in months,

her limbs dancing like the barren arms of a tree reaching
out to snatch a balloon from the wind as it passes.

ON THE WAY TO CALIFORNIA

We drove straight through. Five people, one minivan, and a miniature poodle. I had to keep pulling the blanket my stepmom crocheted for me up to cover my nose, blocking the smoke my dad and stepmom aimed half-heartedly toward cracked windows. Between bouts of yelling, a much louder silence stretching across the car. Someone made a joke about how quiet I was. I fumbled with the gaps in the yarn, trying to push them closed. At midnight, as we passed through L.A., everyone but me was asleep and dad had me sitting next to him up front. He was playing "From the Air" by Laurie Anderson loud enough to drown the traffic and, somehow, no one else woke up. I was supposed to keep my eyes open, so he wouldn't be alone. Never since have my eyelids been so heavy. A decade later, I walk through the streets of the town where I was born and he died and someone might pass by carrying the same phantom smell of nicotine and aftershave. And I might stop, like the flash of a lighter in the rain, or a cigarette still burning on cement.

LAURA

She thinks her hair looks too much like a lion's mane.

She wears winter caps, drinks coffee, and apologizes whenever I show up at her office unannounced while she is eating a salad, or guiding one of her actual students through another painful English 101 essay. I wait with my poems in the hallway for her edits.

Past my dim reflection in the window I can see dot-like people scraping ice off the dashboards of their toy cars.

She notices I haven't slept, the air punched from my lungs to the bags beneath my eyes. She knows I'm lying when I say *I'm alright*, that she needs to drive me to another professional, page through a magazine in the waiting room until I come back out.

We walk down the stairs, each of us putting on our best sense of humor for the sake of the other. We stop to talk under the roof outside, freezing rain pouring down around us. She tells me to send her a text when I get home safe, and promises her doors will be open if I don't.

I fill my hands with her kindnesses. They rattle like change in my pockets everywhere I go.

I see myself in the mirror above the steering wheel before I pull away. The face of someone who's stumbled onto an undeserved wealth. The windshield wipers come on, and the puddles smile a pooled mixture of red and yellow light while another rush hour picks up speed on top of them.

THE VANISHING ACT
(October 11, 1963)

Slide a mascara wand over your eyes
and make the world disappear. Apply
layers of concealer, until no one can
touch your skin. When they ask about

your father, say he moved out of town.
Became a detective. Lawyer. Astronaut.

On his birthday, clench your jaw.
Wait in the car an extra fifteen minutes,
until each swollen trace is removed
from your cheekbones.

Relight your disposition like a candle.

Sometimes, they will look at your face
and say how pretty it has gotten. Sometimes
you will remember to smile. How silly:

these living people, and their habits
of putting makeup on the dead.

MY ONLY SUNSHINE

The sun kisses him and leaves freckles
dotted across his cheekbones,
tiny pieces of her golden glow. Before
I met him, I too pressed my lips
to bodies and bottles
that couldn't hold me tight enough
to still my bones as they shivered
into each other. I fell in love daily. Four times
before breakfast. It is the most beautiful
method of forgetting yourself.

I smiled at strangers, noticed
the looks they gave their shoelaces
at bus stops and empty diner booths. I prayed
they would open their hands, as if
giving something away
could somehow make me whole.

The sun falls on everything equally. Is there
anything lonelier than this
arms' length admiration? By six a.m.,
she is splintering herself through our half-drawn
blinds, and calling it a morning. At noon
she fits perfectly beneath my thumb. I imagine
I am holding her up. I tell her
I've been thinking too much about what
will happen if he leaves me. If I'll rise next to her
in the East. End up in one of those big cities

where no one looks at each other
and smog chokes the clouds. She tells me
how much she envies our artificial bulbs. Those
who flirt with destruction, then get
to burn out, eventually, without the freezing over
of an entire planet on their conscience.

Guilt, she says, *will trick you into life
if you let it.* So I do. But is there anything
lonelier than this page? Everywhere
I go there are stage lights
on my neck, and the play is still going
as she dips down below the curtain of horizon.
We breathe with our eyes closed
in her lukewarm grip. I wake up
with his arms around me. My face inches
from the wall. He says he loves me. I ask why.

IN THE SMOKE

At the restaurant, I take a butter knife and start
sawing through the pages of *The Bell Jar*, surprised
by how easily it cuts. Then I slip the butter knife into my purse.
Two weeks ago, Connie said she was angry at Sylvia
for quitting before she could write another. Laura gasped,
said we weren't allowed to feel anything but sympathy.
All day I fantasize about tearing each page from its spine,
folding them into bite-sized pieces and swallowing them,
one by one, alone at the kitchen table. Then I'd write
a new novel, about myself in disguise. My doppelganger's name
will also have six letters. She will wear big sun hats tied
with pink ribbons, especially on afternoons when it is so
overcast she couldn't see the sky. And whatever room
she is in, no matter how lovely, she will always stand
with one foot out the door. People will think
they know her, the way those who've lived in a big city
all their lives think they are better than the tourists. At night,
she will hold two portraits of her lover and while kissing one
will burn the other, and if anyone asks her why she cries,
she'll stop, sudden as a car horn across the blur of traffic.

ON SLEEPING ALONE

After crying herself quieter than the night-lit cobblestone
of the Spanish side street two stories below our room,
she lays down to stare at the plastered ceiling. She speaks
like dominoes. The other women, the screaming, their last
phone call. Her sixteen-year-old daughter's quiet
disappointment. A round of party calls rises in through
the window she opens every morning, pulling back
its white lace curtains like the lips of her smile. She tells me
she used to be happy. Outside, the car boomerangs away
leaving tire tracks lingering loud as a burnt receiver.
She asks what I would do. A melatonin tablet sinking
to the pit of my stomach as I try to imagine the man
who ironed the music out of her voice, I ball my hands to
fists against the linen bedsheets. I tell her *I'd leave him*.
She laughs, shuts off the light, and turns onto her side. *No*,
she says. *You wouldn't. That's not how we've learned to love.*

WHAT THE PARK BENCH MIGHT HAVE SEEN

heels click   a man sits on a box to play
an accordion for tips he won't receive   arms
widening like the wings of the birds

playing hopscotch around crumbs dropped
from hands of children

a girl who is seventeen years of yearning
of silence of forgetting how to speak
is writing with her head bent as though it

means sometimes   pen racing past
*   everything beautiful she has ever held*
in her hand   and let go by mistake

too fascinated by the floor to realize
she was swooping too low for flying

COST TO DINE

The man outside the cathedral
in Salamanca paces up and down
the cobblestone.

One hand rests on his stomach
concaving beneath
a thin t-shirt, the other reaches

out to us like an empty wine glass.
Por favor, por favor. We walk past

him with the tour, get in line to pay
three and a half euros
so we can climb up the narrow stairs

of the bell tower, snapping photo
after photo of the broad ceilings,
long gold and red carpets, everything

quiet. On our way
back down, the window panes widen

toward sun

like the arms of the clay figure pinned
to a cross on the wall, so thin his ribs
rise to the surface,

pressing, the bell just beginning to toll.

CLIPBOARDS AND PILLS
after Alex Hatter

Lucy's window faces a brick wall.

The nurses, circling every quarter hour with clipboards and pills, keep it locked. They all have these big, young eyes and even younger names: Heather, Emily, Katie. Snapping gum in the backs of their mouths, they give Lucy new names, too: sweetie, honey, dear.

Lucy doesn't mind. She does the same thing to the seagulls outside, as she tosses down slices of Wonder Bread.

Twice a day, the nurses wheel her down the hall to a room with a pool table where she watches a ball white as the outsides of eggs slide back and forth. In the corner, a record player recites lyrics Lucy used to sing, leaned up against a jukebox, blonde hair brushing just past her shoulders.

Now even the titles are fading—worn out as dates on the backs of dirty nickels.

Lucy has holes in her pockets.

Change keeps slipping through them.

Her husband, Victor, once hummed this song into her ear while they half-waltzed around the refrigerator, bodies pinned together at the chest. A prima ballerina in the safety of her own kitchen, Lucy always imagined lights brighter than the glow from the oven.

Victor was a good love to her for seventy-five years. Even as she stopped recognizing him, he kept visiting. But when the nurses said it would be best not to upset her, Victor agreed.

It would be best to remember only the music.

As a gift, he left behind a jewelry box. Showed her how winding it up made the small dancer inside turn. And she liked it. *Her name's Lucy*, he said.

And the nurses let her keep it.

Most of the time, it's quiet: the lid closed, when they wheel her back to the empty bedroom, lean her head against a pillow. But Lucy doesn't dream.

She sleeps—eight hours a night—her mind just can't hold onto images for that long anymore, what with all the spinning.

When it's dark enough for the Heathers, Emilys and Katies to be gone, Lucy pirouettes over the sheets, turning circles like chalk outlines. She knows the concrete is only eight stories away, that it opens and closes under the footsteps of strangers. Knows one day, if she times it right, they will stop for her. But not today.

Today Lucy wakes to the sound of birds, and smiles. She knows they'll still fly in a V, long after it stops standing for anything.

PART FOUR

PLASTIC CUPS

At the funeral, everyone says *We have got
to stop meeting like this* and I nod and I'm still
dizzy, even with the plastic cup of orange punch
my mom said would help, and my love on my arm
which everyone always says will help.
All of his colleagues are here, every realtor in town,
but his children aren't selling the vacant house
of his body. Not yet. It will be cremated later,
scattered into a landscape. His baby grandson
doesn't know he should be crying, and instead
is crawling up the stairs. Everyone talking
over each other—radios tuned to different stations.
I don't know which of these people are relatives,
and which are just tourists here. Trays of croissants,
dips, almonds. Tall men in suits. Women in heels.
The room is full.

LAST PACK OF CIGARETTES

If springtime ever breaks over Browne's Addition
and thaws the sleet and snow from those streets
lined with refurbished mansions the city
divided to rent out as apartments
     you occupied at various points in your life,
an exposed pack of cigarettes will sit on the pavement.

Maybe a squirrel will appear then
and nibble through the packaging.
Get sick from so much man-made poison
—die, even. Then we would have to bury
the squirrel next to your ashes.
Next winter, the snow would cover you
both, everything coming full circle.

The squirrel won't know
that was supposed to have been
your very last pack.

It won't remember me in cloud-print pajamas
racing down the block, inhaling icicles, snow boots
with no socks, hair stringy and stuck to my face
    after you said to bury them
        somewhere you'd never find.
Or how my hands turned pink and raw
digging through ice.

        It won't know about us at all.
We will try to convince ourselves
we are bigger

    more significant
than the squirrel, as though we are not
just as small,
just as alone. Memories get heavier the day
we realize we are the only ones still trying to lift them.

AFTER A HALF BOTTLE OF KRAKEN

Just before daybreak and we are laying with our backs
to the cooling summer asphalt. I feel the sky trapping us

inside the glass rinse jar of a brooding artist swirling clean
the blue from her brush when I tell him I've considered

it. And he pulls me in close and quiet as a bridge dive
into the river snaking our city in two. *But I won't*, I say.

But you wouldn't, he says. And we almost find peace
there, before he lifts us back to our feet and leads me

through Peaceful Valley to his couch where I sleep alone
and the cushions feel like vertigo. When I close my eyes

I imagine the scene from *The Bell Jar* when Esther sits
at the cusp between rock and water, everything calming.

And I wonder about the ocean: if it ever swallows itself,
or just imagines the taste often enough to forget it hasn't.

WINDOWS AS WALLS

This morning I drove past a car accident
on the way to school—smoke still coming up
from the two engine claws torn apart from
their kiss. And I slowed way down to see if anyone
was crying, what shapes the twisted metal
was making. Sometimes I worry that
staring at one crash while walking toward
another will catch up to me. I am always
floating to doors on the ends of long hallways
turning round and round like corkscrews
in front of me. And the therapist asks me why
I don't kill myself and I tell her about the love
but not the fear, because I don't know which
is stronger anymore. And she nods, asks
how I'm sleeping. I wake up an hour before
my alarm goes off, turn over to face the wall.
I climb the stairs and look out over the sink
past the petals of withering flowers given to me
on Valentine's Day and think about tiny insects
crawling across the leaves. *Not enough*, I say.

A POEM FOR THE UNINSPIRED

When the year's first yellow tulip
in a planter outside the window of Shari's
on Monroe and Northwest Boulevard

looks at you wrong,

cut off its head. Tape the petals
over your eyes and either

sleep
or pretend to,

it doesn't make much of a difference
as long as you are dreaming.

HAMARTIA

Gutter ball. A swing and a miss. He shoots. *Folks, it's all downhill from here.* The crowd weeps. The hero trips. From the very last step of the ladder, he falls. *What a shame*, they curse. And cry. *What a pity*. Perhaps, it is like my mother in her 20s. Tired of being called pretty, she cut her hair to the least flattering angle just to see who still saw her. Certainly, those clumps of hair like dust on the tile might have looked a tragedy to someone, but not to her. Perhaps, while we shiver alongside barren tree limbs, they let go willingly. At last released from the tight clutches of vanity.

SECOND DEGREE BLACK BELT

Even as I stood there
       a young girl scanning the crowd for her father
I knew the moment was too cliché, that I might spend

the rest of my life clawing out of its frame.
I'd find out later
he was busy bailing his friend from jail. I'd tie that belt

around my waist
tight, like a ring around a rolled napkin,
pat dry his apology, and wonder

       how many times I'd have to do this *turn,
jump, and kick*   through a stack of three boards
before the hands of every clapping spectator would break.

DUST ON THE FRAME

My father points a disposable Kodak camera at my face
in front of the house on Belt where he lives across the street
from an always empty church parking lot. I smile on instinct,
even though my hair is matted, and my pajama pants

are too short for my beanstalk legs. *Don't smile*, he says.
*Unless you are really that happy. Otherwise, when you look
      back at this, it will be a lie.* There is a photo of him
in my kitchen drawer from our trip to California. It's January,

but you wouldn't know it from the sunlight reflecting
off his balding head six feet and four inches above the ground
where he stands over a Hollywood cement star. Even there

in the ninety-degree heat, he kept his leather jacket
      plastered to his skin.   I realize he must have
         been smiling. I realize
I am starting to forget him.

CRUMBLING ARCHITECTURE

You can still drive past his old apartment building. Squint at the numbers through the dark to be sure. You can even walk up to the door. Push it open into a moment that no longer exists. Climb the ladder into someone else's bunk bed. Close your eyes and listen for the orchestra of a city at night: echoes of breaking glass and car horns. You can awaken to the swinging of a screen door, the lighting of his morning cigarette. You can drag your feet across the carpet to the place where his wooden chair left its indentation in the fabric and cradle your knees to your chest rocking back and forth you can claw chunks of skin from your arms and legs and search your flesh for the details of an unraveling memory

don't forget about the spaces
in your mind that continue to bleed when
poked like undercooked meat

                              You can still drive past his
                              old apartment building.

don't forget that he won't be there
no matter how many times you knock
or how much you plead

                              The walls will be repainted.

don't forget how every room
empties after enough days have
rotated outside of its windows

                              The car in front will be new.

don't forget the crumbling architecture
of every great city how everyone collapses
eventually everything decays

Don't forget how everything ends.

don't   forget   how   everything

    ends   don't forget

everything ends

                                      don't

forget everything

WHAT THE WALLPAPER MIGHT HAVE SEEN

an open bedroom window   swirling
patterns like braille across the ceiling
while he snores a gentle machinery

    she lets him sleep while he can
how exhausting it must be to love someone
so preoccupied with hating themselves

    makes peace with the rustling sheets
and begs the quiet place behind her eyelids

to believe the next time they open
she will be different

COMMUNITY COLLEGE
for Laura Read

       I don't know what it is about this place, but on the walk
across campus to my car, parked in the only spot
marked with stones like a grave, there is a clock without hands.
       It's set high up on a brick tower, silent as building seven
where I take two separate yoga classes in the same day.

       I don't know what it is
about pain, but three weeks ago I listened to Sherman Alexie
read a few of his poems. Before he went on stage, students
from the Salish School read their stories
    off notecards. One girl was talking about her mother's
alcoholism. About halfway through, she stopped and ran
        behind the curtain and the audience only stared.

       I don't know much about
anything. But it is the last day of May and I am allergic
to the air. I am in love and lonely, home and homesick, restless
       and exhausted. Some people are clocks without hands.
There is nothing pointing us toward north, no one to set us forward,
        or adjust to the seasonal shifts. You can wind us up
all you want. We do not always come here to chime.

AND THE FEVER AND THE CHILLS
for Tim Johnson

And the carousel kept spinning
while I sat on the bench outside it,
a book about existentialism
on my lap. The women gave me
knowing looks, pushed their strollers
a little further away. I fantasized
about stealing babies. I'd pick two
and, clutching one against each of my
breasts, I'd say *Just try taking
little Anna and Christopher from me.*
The wooden horses went up and down
with the organ music. Screaming
children posed for photos,
their teeth dyed with snow cones.
I don't know how many August
afternoons I spent there, paying dollar
after dollar so the fortune teller, Zoltar,
who lived inside a machine could
spit out little slips of cardboard
reassuring me I was destined
for greatness, wealth, and happiness
happiness happiness. I caught
glimpses of myself in the mirror
at the carousel's center: hair unwashed,
bright red lipstick pursed
into a frown. If it wasn't moving quite
so fast, I'd rush up and kiss
the reflection before curling my hands
into fists. I'd punch until my knuckles

bled and the families would finally
understand, pile into minivans
and go back home for the week.
But the carousel kept spinning
and the old men stared at my dress
and the grass outside went yellow.

NOT ANOTHER GRIEF POEM

Our dead do not sleep sound.
Like candles melting in the middle of the day
or garden hoses left running in the rain.
      I haven't visited a grave in months,
so the holes have started coming to me.

To grieve is to spend years leveling
a ditch, with shovels full of nothing.
We keep digging, because we must,

when every song of redemption seems
to echo through the same hollow chords,
we dig; when decorations in cemeteries
start making the headstones look bigger,

we dig, because our initials may be carved
into granite before we learn to trust the bark
of a tree to keep them bonded to a lovers'.

We dig bags out from under our eyes: six
feet and only getting deeper, because our dead
do not sleep sound. So neither do we.

I've got this rustling in my closet like restless
suit coats, or nooses. When I try to open the door
a crack, its knob comes loose in my hand

like ashes tipped from an urn in the shape
of my father. In his arms, he carries a cardboard
box of artifacts:

Grandma Rain's turtle brooches. Grandfather's
Frisbees. Uncle Chuck's adjustable baseball caps.
Nana's yellow bird. Papa's dog tags. The locket
my sister wears around her neck, a piece of hair
      from a baby girl clamped tight inside.

And he is leaving. And I can't keep up
with his strides. Otherwise, I would leave this all
behind in a heartbeat. Find my family and ask why,
      in the nightmares, as I watch them
die again in slow motion,
            I am the only one still fighting.

But our dead do not sleep sound,
so I tear pages from the scalps of notebooks
for not letting the past lay flat

and quiet as bones. I write, *Not another*
grief poem, pulled like flagged rope from
a magician's crooked teeth.

I am seventeen years old and already the soil
           is reaching up at my ankles. So I run
faster, forget the hymns of what is fair
      and what is wrong; of those I loved
and all I've lost. I will never go far enough

to shake my own shadow. The living don't always wake up.
Sometimes, we hover, shovels in our arms,
and like on autopilot, we dig and dig and dig, working in rows
beneath that heavy sun. We feel our weary chins
      lift, and somehow, can bring ourselves to whistle.

ACKNOWLEDGEMENTS

"Crumbling Architecture" first appeared in *Riverlit No. 13: Volume 4, Issue 1*

A version of "Grandfather Rabbit" first appeared in *The Floating Bridge Review #7*

"The Past Twelve Minutes" first appeared in the 2014 edition of *The Wire Harp*

"My Dad's Favorite Supertramp Album", "And the Fever and the Chills", and "Not Another Grief Poem" first appeared in *Drunk in A Midnight Choir*

"In the Smoke" first appeared in *Riverlit No. 17: Volume 5, Issue 1*

AUTHOR'S NOTE

There is not nearly enough page space to thank everyone who deserves to be mentioned. Because of this, it is my intention to continue showing my gratitude to all of you, as I work toward becoming the type of person deserving of the grace you have shown me.

In a very direct sense, this book owes much of itself to Laura and Sean. Thank you both for believing in me from the beginning. Without your guidance and encouragement, it is likely this would still be an overwhelming pile of unsorted sheets of paper on the floor. I would also like to thank Tyler for the intuitive and constructive care he took with editing this manuscript, as well as Greg for welcoming me into the University of Hell family.

On the note of families, I would also like to mention my biological one. To my extended family, thank you: I cannot imagine this book was an easy read, but please know how much I love you. Mom, Allie, and Grant, we will always be in the same boat, even while it is sinking.

I would like to thank Isaac, and the rest of the nurturing community leaders in Spokane. Mark, thank you for loving me when I did not love myself. Kurt, thank you for reminding me of all the things worth rushing besides death. Tim, thank you for the piece of paper you once put in the pocket of a leather jacket.

Claire, my lovely soul-twin, thank you for the beautiful illustrations.

And lastly, a giant hug to anyone and everyone who has ever experienced magic at a certain burrito shop on First Avenue.

ABOUT THE AUTHOR

Lauren Gilmore was born in Spokane, Washington on the autumnal equinox of 1996. Since then, she has written poems, stories, and love letters, some of which have been read and published by other people. *Outdancing the Universe* is her first book. She is now working toward translating the word "butterfly" into every language.

Author Photograph by Amia

THIS BOOK IS ONE OF THE MANY AVAILABLE FROM UNIVERSITY OF HELL PRESS. DO YOU HAVE THEM ALL?

by Tyler Atwood
an electric sheep jumps to greener pasture

by John W Barrios
Here Comes the New Joy

by Eirean Bradley
the I in team
the little BIG book of Go Kill Yourself

by Calvero
someday i'm going to marry Katy Perry
i want love so great it makes Nicholas Sparks cream in his pants

by Leah Noble Davidson
Poetic Scientifica
Door

by Rory Douglas
The Most Fun You'll Have at a Cage Fight

by Brian S. Ellis
American Dust Revisited
Often Go Awry

by Greg Gerding
The Burning Album of Lame
Venue Voyeurisms: Bars of San Diego
Loser Makes Good: Selected Poems 1994
Piss Artist: Selected Poems 1995-1999
The Idiot Parade: Selected Poems 2000-2005

by Robert Duncan Gray
Immaculate/The Rhododendron and Camellia Year Book (1966)

by Joseph Edwin Haeger
Learn to Swim

by Lindsey Kugler
HERE.

by Wryly T. McCutchen
My Ugly and Other Love Snarls

by Michael McLaughlin
Countless Cinemas

by Johnny No Bueno
We Were Warriors
Don't

by A.M. O'Malley
What to Expect When You're Expecting Something Else

by Stephen M. Park
High & Dry
The Grass is Greener

by Christine Rice
Swarm Theory

by Michael N. Thompson
A Murder of Crows
Days of Swine and Roses

by Sarah Xerta
Nothing to Do with Me

UNIVERSITY OF HELL PRESS

*Denting the world with words,
one incendiary book at a time.*

CPSIA information can be obtained at www.ICGtesting.com
Printed in the USA
BVOW07s1944100615

403986BV00004B/4/P